HOOD RIVER VALLEY
LAND OF PLENTY

Peter, Janet and Beautiful America Publishing want to thank the sponsors listed below, for their support and assistance in making this book possible. Our thanks to all. Enjoy.

———————————— ◆ ————————————

STERNWHEELER COLUMBIA GORGE

HOOD RIVER INN

TIMBERLINE LODGE

COOPER SPUR MOUNTAIN RESORT

WAUCOMA BOOKSTORE

RE/MAX RESULTS, INC., REALTORS

HOOD RIVER VALLEY
LAND OF PLENTY

PHOTOGRAPHY BY PETER MARBACH

TEXT BY JANET COOK

Peter Marbach

Beautiful America Publishing Company

Mt. Hood from Lost Lake in fall

Cover photograph: Mt. Hood and the Hood River Valley

Published by
Beautiful America Publishing Company
P.O. Box 244
Woodburn, OR 97071
www.beautifulamericapub.com

Library of Congress Catalog Number 2003019082

ISBN 0-89802-768-3
ISBN 0-89802-769-1 (paperback)

Printed in Korea

A beautiful sunset in the Columbia River Gorge from Hood River

TABLE OF CONTENTS

CHAPTER 1

AN EMBARRASSMENT OF RICHES

There are few places on Earth that stir passion in people's souls like the Hood River Valley. Stretching from the steep glaciers of Mt. Hood to the shores of the Columbia River, the Hood River Valley is a 25-mile-long wonder tucked into the Cascade Mountain Range of northern Oregon. Its geologic past is a story of tumultuous upheavals and rending cataclysms, as Mt. Hood's eruptions over millennia sent lava and ash tumbling from the volcano down the valley floor. Other massive natural forces, from prehistoric earthquakes to the giant ice age floods that created the Columbia River and its famous gorge, combined over millions of years to create what today is one of the great valleys of the world.

The Hood River Valley cradles some of the richest agricultural land on earth. More than 220,000 tons of pears, apples and cherries are produced annually in the valley's 15,000 acres of orchards. Half of all winter pears grown in the United States are grown here, and the valley is one of the leading Anjou pear growing regions in the world. The Hood River Valley Newtown Pippin apple is considered the highest quality Pippin grown anywhere. Sweet cherries round out the valley's top three crops, and a burgeoning wine grape industry is emerging.

But its bounty reaches far beyond the fruit that grows so abundantly here. The valley's stunning scenery and boundless recreational opportunities have captivated people for more than a century and, more recently, have lured a whole generation of outdoor enthusiasts who came here to play, and stayed. There are few places in the world where there are so many recreational opportunities in so small an area. The 35 miles from Mt. Hood to

Paul Wang's Asian Pears, Odell

Organic Gala Apples, Mt. Hood Organic Farms

Hood River Bing Cherries

8

Trail running in the Hood River Valley

Men's freestyle surfing, Gorge Games

Julio Via Monte, Telemark skier

the Columbia River practically overwhelms with options: skiing, snowboarding, snowshoeing, hiking, mountain climbing, camping, fishing, mountain biking, kayaking, canoeing, horseback riding, wakeboarding, windsurfing and kiteboarding. Hood River was made famous by windsurfing, but the valley is a true recreationist's paradise.

And, of course, it's the people here who help to complete the cornucopia of the Hood River Valley. In a region of the country that's notoriously homogenous, the Hood River Valley is home to large communities of people from diverse ethnic and cultural backgrounds, including Finns, Germans, Japanese and Hispanics. They have all brought their own unique traditions to life in the valley, enriching all who live here and visit.

Here, in a few dozen square miles, are fantastic contrasts. There are temperate, sea-level beaches and alpine glaciers, lush rainforest and barren, desert hillsides. In less than 20 miles, annual rainfall varies more than 100 inches. A sophisticated small city is just minutes from remote wilderness. It is a place of stunning vistas, towering mountains, cascading waterways, prolific fruit, legendary wind, pastoral countryside and diverse people. Those who live here are fiercely proud of their valley. Those who visit long to take a piece of it home. And who could blame them? The Hood River Valley is a treasure of the world. It is geography writ large. It is a land of plenty.

Chapter 2

Take It From The Top

Any story about the Hood River Valley must really begin at the top, with 11,240-foot Mt. Hood. Towering at the south end of the valley like a sentinel, Mt. Hood is the highest mountain in Oregon and the fourth-highest peak of the 700-mile long Cascade Range stretching from northern California to southern British Columbia. Like a monolithic Mona Lisa, Mt. Hood seems to peek at Oregonians in all corners of the state, looming at astonishing angles from far west of Portland, from the southern reaches of the Willamette Valley, and from the high desert of eastern Oregon. But she saves her most dazzling face for the valley below her that bears her name.

Native Americans who lived along the Columbia River for 10,000 years before white men arrived called the mountain Wy'East. In the summer, they hiked from their riverside villages to the high alpine meadows below the mountain's glaciers to hunt, to pick huckleberries and harvest roots, and to peel bark from cedar trees for weaving into baskets. Indian trails that rose from the river through the valley to the mountain were later used by pioneers who homesteaded in the upper valley. Today, some of those same ancient trails are the modern roads of the valley, while others are recreation trails meandering through wilderness, changed little from pre-modern times.

The Indians were the first human witnesses to Mt. Hood's volcanic fury. Mt. Hood and the nearby Cascade peaks were so boisterous that the Native Americans' legend about the mountains was passed down through generations, and eventually on to the white settlers who began arriving in the mid-1800s. The legend had it that two warrior brothers, Wy'East and Pa-Toe

Following two pages: Mt. Hood summit with Mt. Jefferson in the distance

(Mt. Adams, directly north from Mt. Hood across the Columbia River), were both in love with beautiful Squaw Mountain. She loved Wy'East, but flirted with Pa-Toe and the brothers fought viciously, spewing lava and hurling rocks and fire at one another. The battle raged on and off over time, burning the valley and forests, frightening the people and cutting a huge river valley between the mountains. Squaw Mountain began slipping away at night from her guardian, an old woman named Loo-Wit, to be with Wy'East. One morning, Pa-Toe saw her sneaking back from Wy'East and his jealous rage started the battle all over again. Loo-Wit tried to stop the destruction, but she was old and weak. The Great Spirit, father of the warrior brothers, watched in sadness. He rewarded Loo-Wit for trying to stop the battle by granting her wish for youth. Then he set her apart from his sons and she can be seen today as the youngest of the Cascade Mountains, Mt. St. Helens. Pa-Toe claimed Squaw Mountain as his own. But she was broken-hearted and soon fell at Pa-Toe's feet, sinking into a deep sleep from which she never awoke. Pa-Toe, once tall and proud like Wy'East, was anguished by what had happened, dropped his head in shame and never raised it again.

When Lewis and Clark came through the area in 1805 on their journey to the Pacific Ocean – and later when white settlers arrived in Hood River – they were warned by the Indians of the fury of the "sleeping giants." But Mt. Hood and the nearby Cascade volcanoes remained docile and the stories went mostly ignored. Indeed, the last major eruption of Mt. Hood was in 1790 – 15 years before Lewis and Clark passed through. The mountain has been relatively quiet ever since, with only sporadic and minor belching coming from its upper reaches.

Mt. Hood's recent dormancy is part of why the north face of the mountain towering above the Hood River Valley remains its most dramatic. The 1790 eruption sent lava flowing down the mountain's west side, leaving intact the symmetrical cone and the dramatic contours etched by earlier ice ages on the north face. In 1937, Oregon mountaineer and journalist Fred McNeil described Mt. Hood as giving us the "happy paradox of an unchanging object that never looks the same." Nowhere is that more true than in the Hood River Valley. But McNeil was only partly right; the mountain has been outwardly unchanging for a couple of centuries now, but vents and fumaroles exhaling a sulfur-smelling steam high on the peak attest to the fact that Mt. Hood is very much alive. In fact, the mountain is thought to be one of the most potentially dangerous volcanoes in the Cascades, in part because it lies so close to a major metropolitan area. History has indicated that Mt. Hood tends to erupt in cycles with Mt. St. Helens, which famously blew its top in May 1980 – a nanosecond ago in geologic time. Still, scientists predict that the next major eruption on Mt. Hood will affect mostly the weaker southwest side of the cone, with minimal repercussions to the Hood River Valley. Then again, nature doesn't always abide by man's wishes.

Despite the potential volatility of Mt. Hood – or perhaps because those who love the mountain know it will one day change forever, quite possibly in their lifetime–it is a beloved year-round recreation haven. Mt. Hood's natural wonderland offers something to everyone, whether it's hiking to a thundering glacier waterfall, camping in an alpine meadow filled with wildflowers, climbing to the peak's summit, mountain biking through moss-laden forest, snowshoeing through

Mt. Hood and the Hood River Valley from Highway 35

16

A beautiful farm with a great backdrop

towering stands of fir and pine, or skiing at one of the mountain's ski areas. The Mt. Hood National Forest spans 1.2 million acres, nearly half of those on the north side of the mountain and descending into the upper Hood River Valley. Within these forest boundaries lies the 47,000-acre Mt. Hood Wilderness Area, which encompasses some of the most pristine wild lands in the Northwest.

CHAPTER 3

A MOUNTAIN PLAYGROUND

M t. Hood was discovered as a recreation mecca soon after emigrants began arriving off the Oregon Trail in the mid-1800s. Climbing the mountain became an obsession for some of the first settlers. The first officially documented climb to the peak's summit took place in 1857 when a party from Portland, led by newspaperman Henry Pittock, scaled the mountain's south side. Since then, the mountain has been climbed countless times. Today, more than 10,000 people register to climb Mt. Hood every year, making it the most climbed snow-clad peak in the United States and second in the world only to Japan's Mt. Fuji. There are nearly a dozen established routes to the top, all of them requiring technical gear and expertise. Most climbers opt for the easier routes on the mountain's south side. But ever since some early Hood River Valley mountaineers first found their way to the top on "their" side of the mountain in the 1800s, many intrepid souls have tackled the difficult north face routes.

The north face of Mt. Hood, with its dramatic vistas, has long intrigued those living in the Hood River Valley below. Only 30 years after the first settlers arrived in Hood River, when there were still only primitive roads leading up the valley, several enterprising residents began planning a resort high on the mountain's north flank. In 1884, four Hood Riverites set off through the mountain wilderness in search of a location near timberline where they could establish a summer camp. They gathered laborers to cut a primitive road through the steep, thick forest, and the next year a tent camp was established at 6,000 feet, just below Eliot Glacier. The camp was the first snowline

Mt. Hood from the deck of Cloud Cap Inn

Crag Rats plan the best route for a rescue mission

Crag Rats on snow dome ski into action

A well-earned rest at Cloud Cap Inn

21

"resort" with guest accommodations on any peak in the Northwest.

The journey up the valley to the camp by stage was long and arduous – requiring several changes of horses – and after initial success, guest numbers soon dwindled. By 1888 two Portland men who had become enamored of the camp acquired the road and property rights and went about making improvements to both. They began building a timber lodge on a rock promontory near the site of the old tent camp. Giant firs were felled three miles below and hauled up a 22 percent grade to the building site. Rock blasted from nearby cliffs was used to build two great fireplaces. The rough-hewn timber logs were bolted together one by one and, upon completion, the entire structure was anchored by steel cables to the rock on which it stood.

The Cloud Cap Inn opened in 1889 as the first alpine resort in the West. Many in the Hood River Valley, and elsewhere, doubted whether the inn could withstand the howling winds and heavy snows that pummel the mountain during winter. In February of 1890, two Hood River Valley men set out on cross country skis in the first recorded ski trip up Mt. Hood's north side to find out what fate might have befallen the inn. When they arrived two days later, they found that snow had drifted inside, but otherwise the building was unscathed.

Cloud Cap enjoyed a steady stream of summer guests well into the early 1920s and was the pride of the Hood River Valley. But construction of hotels on the south side of the mountain – and completion of the Mt. Hood Loop Road in 1925, which provided easy access to the south side of the mountain – signaled the beginning of the end for the Cloud Cap Inn. The Great Depression ended a funding drive for upgrading the road to Cloud Cap, and though the road later was improved, it was too late. In 1940 the Forest Service purchased the empty inn and soon boarded it up. By the 1950s, they had plans to demolish the building, but a Hood River-based search and rescue group offered to take over responsibility for the inn's upkeep in exchange for using it as a base for training and mountain rescues. In 1974, Cloud Cap Inn was placed on Oregon's official Registry of Historic Places. Although it's undergone several renovations over the years, the inn that many doubted could withstand one Mt. Hood winter has now stood for 114 of them.

Climbing, exploring and camping on Mt. Hood was getting so popular by the early 1900s that a group of Hood River Valley residents who climbed frequently together felt the need to form a search and rescue group. A search for a lost boy in 1923 brought the idea to the forefront again. Then, in 1926, another hunt for a lost boy brought out searchers from the Forest Service, Portland-based mountaineering clubs, the U.S. Army, and police from both Portland and Hood River. The Hood River Valley climbers joined the search and, after several days, they found the boy deep in the woods surviving on huckleberries. When the men delivered the boy safely to his family, reporters asked which search group they were from. The men did some fast thinking and came up with the Crag Rats from the words used by the wife of one of the members to describe the men after a day climbing among the crags of Mt. Hood.

The Crag Rats soon became a well-known search and rescue group on the mountain, and often traveled to other Cascade peaks in Oregon and Washington to aid in searches. It was the Crag Rats who helped to save Cloud Cap Inn from demolition, and they have used it as a base for rescue operations for nearly

Skier on Polallie snow field, high above Cooper Spur ski area

The fabulous Cooper Spur Ski Resort

50 years. The Crag Rats maintain and do upgrades to the historic building, and watch over it with a fierce loyalty. Today the Crag Rats are recognized as the oldest search and rescue organization in the country. About 25 of the 100 or so members are very active in search and rescue operations on Mt. Hood year-round, and are frequently sought out for their expertise on mountain safety and mountaineering in general. The Crag Rats still wear the signature black and white checkered shirts that they've worn since the 1920s, and many a lucky soul lost or stranded on Mt. Hood has seen the arrival of men – and women – in that shirt and known salvation.

Climbing wasn't the only activity that got an early start on Mt. Hood. Nearly a decade before Timberline Lodge was built on the south side of the mountain to serve skiers, climbers and tourists from Portland, Hood River Valley residents were making a ski hill in their own back yard on the mountain's north side. In 1927, a property owner on the mountain's northeast flank suggested to members of a local ski club that they build a ski jump on his land. A swath was cleared through the woods and Jump Hill, as it was known for decades, opened that winter and became popular with Hood River Valley skiers for its convenience.

The area underwent small expansions over the next couple of decades, including the addition of a short tow rope. In 1950, the ski club enlisted the help of local orchardists who hauled farm equipment up to the area to clear more runs. A warming hut was built at the base, where it remained until it burned to the ground in a fire in 1996 and has since been replaced. Eventually the rope tow was lengthened, and another one built – both powered by Chrysler engines. By the 1960s ski racers and jumpers from the

Hood River Valley were flocking to the area, along with a growing number of recreational skiers just getting started in the expanding sport. The area was christened Cooper Spur Ski Area in the late 1960s, and new owners installed a T-bar capable of taking 1,200 skiers per hour to the top of the small area.

Cooper Spur has enjoyed small expansions and improvements during the last quarter century, but has always remained a family-friendly ski area that the Hood River Valley has called its own. Several local kids' ski clubs are based at Cooper Spur, and the area has served as the start for some top regional ski racers. The area also has a sledding hill and is a favorite summer spot for family hiking outings. Cooper Spur was recently bought by Mt. Hood Meadows and several changes are planned, including more chairlifts and expanded terrain.

Mt. Hood Meadows' main ski area, on the south side of the mountain, opened in 1968 and has been a staple for Hood River Valley skiers ever since. The area offers 2,150 acres of skiable terrain, as well as a Nordic center with 15 kilometers of groomed trails for cross-country skating and skiing. On winter mornings in Hood River, skiers and snowboarders can be found at any number of the local coffee shops grabbing some java before heading up to the hill. From coffee shop to chairlift at Meadows takes only 45 minutes. In addition to Cooper Spur and Meadows, Mt. Hood boasts four other ski areas, including Timberline, which holds honors as having the longest ski season in North America. Open through the summer, Timberline's famous Palmer Glacier serves as the off-season training ground for the U.S. Ski Team and is home to several summer snowboard camps. A favorite summer-time activity of Hood River "boardheads" is the Daily Double: ski or snowboard at Timberline in the morning,

Winter in Mt. Hood National Forest

Mt. Hood rises above snowshoer along Newton Creek

then return to Hood River to windsurf in the afternoon. Real outdoor nuts can pull a triple by adding a mountain bike or hike to the day's activities.

The wilderness of Mt. Hood also offers premier cross country and backcountry skiing as well as snowshoeing, for those seeking more solitude than the busy ski areas offer. Cross country skiers find dozens of trails right off Highway 35 – the modern day Loop Road around the mountain – accessed from the many designated winter parking areas (called Sno-Parks). But many of the most spectacular trails are in the upper Hood River Valley – including the Tilly Jane Historic Area, named after the wife of one of the men who built Cloud Cap. In continual use as a recreation area since the 1880s, the Tilly Jane area encompasses thousands of acres between Cooper Spur and the Cloud Cap Inn. The Tilly Jane Trail is a favorite ski and snowshoe trail – albeit a steep one, climbing nearly 2,000 feet in less than three miles. A Forest Service cabin sits at the top of the trail, near the historic Tilly Jane Campground, for use by recreationists. An historic amphitheater at the campground dates to the early 1900s, when Hood River Valley campers would stage shows around a bonfire before rising the next morning to climb Mt. Hood. In addition, many Forest Service roads spanning the flanks of Mt. Hood's north side are open for skiing and snowshoeing. With an average snowfall measuring in the hundreds of inches, Mt. Hood is a winter wonderland for anyone who loves the outdoors.

Along with climbing and skiing on Mt. Hood, there is world-class hiking and mountain biking in the warmer seasons on a seemingly boundless number of trails – all told there are 1,200 miles of trails in the Mt. Hood National Forest. Terrain varies widely from alpine scree fields high above timberline to creek-side trails meandering through dense, moss-laden forest. Depending on where you are on the mountain, tree species and wildflowers vary widely. Douglas fir dominates the lower slopes of Mt. Hood followed, as the elevation rises, by Western Hemlock, Pacific Silver fir, Noble fir, Mountain Hemlock, Subalpine fir and Whitebark pine. Timberline occurs at about 6,500 feet. Closer to the ground, depending on elevation and moisture levels, Oregon grape, salal, rhododendron and devil's club flourish. In fall, the mountain slopes are ablaze with firey red vine maple. In the spring and summer, a menagerie of wild-flowers ranging from bog orchids and monkey flower to lupine and paintbrush sprinkle meadows and hillsides with brilliant color.

Mountain lakes on the peak's north side add still another element to the recreation possibilities on Mt. Hood. Lost Lake, which seems suspended high in the upper reaches of the valley on the northwest flank of the mountain, was used as a camp long before white men arrived in the area. Columbia River Indians used the lake as a base camp during the summer berry picking season. Still, when white men arrived in the Hood River Valley there was no defined trail to the lake – then referred to as Big Lake. In 1880, a group of Hood River men set out to hike to the remote lake. After two days of hacking through dense under-brush, the group arrived at where they thought the lake should be – but wasn't. When the men joked that it was the lake that was lost, not them, the new name stuck.

Around the turn of the century the Forest Service was estab-lishing official campgrounds in response to growing demand for wilderness access. In 1900, Lost Lake Campground was opened as

Tamanawas Falls, a popular day hike

Opposite: Beautiful Lost Lake with Mt. Hood in the distance

one of the first Forest Service campgrounds in the country. At that time, there was still only a primitive road that went from the community of Dee, on the west side of the upper valley, to within a few miles of the lake. By 1910, the Mt. Hood Railroad reached Dee and many campers would take the train from Hood River, then make the trek from Dee on foot. A 1920s Forest Service brochure read, "From Dee the walk to the lake is 14 miles. Good campgrounds are situated about 7 miles from Dee on the Dee-Lost Lake Road. Vigorous hikers will make the trip to Lost Lake the same day."

Today, a two-lane road winds through the forest from Dee right up to the lake's shore. The campground is popular in the summer, and the lake provides a great escape from Hood River and the valley on sweltering summer days. A well-maintained four-mile trail encircles the lake. Along with the campground, several cabins are available for rent, as well as canoes and paddleboats. The view from the northwest shore of Lost Lake across the water to Mt. Hood, with its snow-capped peak reflecting perfectly in the crystal-clear water, is one of the most memorable – and photographed – scenes in Oregon.

Laurance Lake, located a few miles southwest of Parkdale, is actually a reservoir created by the Clear Creek Dam. Steep forested ridges rise on either side of the lake, and Mt. Hood towers to the south. Like its neighbor Lost Lake, Laurance Lake provides a cool summer getaway. The Forest Service maintains a small campground and a boat launch at the lake, and fishing in this alpine setting is a favorite pastime.

CHAPTER 4
THE TRICKLE-DOWN THEORY,
HOOD RIVER VALLEY STYLE

The mountain is central to the story of the Hood River Valley for more than just its prominent position and the recreational opportunities it affords. Mt. Hood, and the surrounding Cascade mountain ridges that punctuate the west side of the valley, create a trio of circumstances that together have made the Hood River Valley what it is today. The first ingredient in this fortuitous recipe evolved over millions of years of volcanic eruptions. The lava, ash and other debris that was tossed from the ever-growing mountain, building up layer after layer in the valley, broke down over time into a mineral rich soil. The ridge of peaks on the west side of the valley – which includes 4,960-foot Mt. Defiance – and the Hood River Fault, the escarpment of which forms the north-south ridge running along the east side of the valley, act to cradle the rich sediments that have been piled between them over thousands of years. In addition to rich soil borne of the mountain, silt deposited along the shores of the prehistoric Columbia River, which once flowed across the valley and around the northwest side of Mt. Hood, added to the black gold that gradually accumulated in the Hood River Valley.

The second auspicious ingredient in the mix is weather. The Hood River Valley sits just to the east of the spine of the Cascade Range in a chasm between rainforest and desert. Within the span of a few miles from west to east, average annual rainfall varies from 130 inches on a ridge near Lost Lake to 45 inches in the upper valley town of Parkdale to just 30 inches in Hood River. The high desert of Eastern Oregon looms to the east; in The Dalles, 17 miles from Hood River, just 15 inches of rain falls

Mt. Hood from Parkdale in the fall

The main branch of Hood River in the fall

annually. Storms rolling in from the Pacific Ocean get tangled in the rugged Cascades, often draping Mt. Hood and the mountains to her west in the winter blanket of clouds and fog that produce the moisture which will sustain the valley through the growing season. In summer, the mountain range serves as a barrier to weaker weather systems, allowing for warm sunny days and cool nights from late spring through fall.

Finally, the mountain acts as a sponge that never dries out. Storms dump an annual average of 150 inches of precipitation on the glaciers that in turn feed a web of streams, creeks and rivers which provide abundant water year-round to the valley below. Trickles that begin far beneath snow-covered fields flow into more than 70 individual waterways that tumble down the north side of Mt. Hood. In all, nearly 600 miles of intermittent streams flood the valley with enough water to nourish thousands of acres of orchards many times over. Much of the water streaming off the mountain eventually runs into one of the three branches of the Hood River. Each branch – the East Fork, the Middle Fork and the West Fork – has its own singular beauty as it tumbles down the valley, swallowing run-off from smaller streams along the way. The East Fork joins the Middle Fork around the valley's distinct landmark Middle Mountain, and it in turn joins the West Fork near picturesque Punchbowl Falls. From there, the Hood River carries much of Mt. Hood's watery gift the rest of the way down the valley and pours it into the Columbia.

CHAPTER 5

A FRUIT GROWER'S PARADISE

Early settlers to the Hood River Valley enjoyed the temperate climate, and used the rushing glacier streams and abundant springs for fishing, drinking and household chores. But it didn't take long for them to realize that their new-found home might also be an agricultural paradise. Hood River's founding father, Nathaniel Coe, arrived in 1854 and planted the first fruit trees the very next year on a portion of his Donation Land Claim in what is now downtown Hood River. He and his family planted apples, pears, apricots, strawberries, peaches and plums. The first recorded sale of fruit came in 1858, when the Coes sold a thousand pounds of peaches in The Dalles. The Coe apple trees began to bear fruit in 1859, and by 1860 the family had nearly 300 trees planted in what was the first of the valley's orchards. But for most of the early years, peaches were what Hood River was known for. The famous Dog River peaches – so called for the early name of Hood River, before Nathaniel Coe's wife, Mary, changed it to Hood River, which she deemed more respectable – were taken by steamer to The Dalles and to Portland, and were known around the Northwest for their sweet, juicy flavor. Growing peaches fell out of favor eventually, when it became apparent that the fruit couldn't stand up to the occasional winter freezes and suffered with the winter rains.

As the town of Hood River grew, people moved up the valley to plant fruit on larger tracts of land. In 1876, Ezra Smith started what became the first commercial orchard in the valley with 30 acres planted in apples. By the 1880s, whole areas of dense forest that had blanketed much of the valley were being cleared for planting, the logs hauled to one of the local mills which were

Pear blossoms, barn and Mt. Hood off the Old Dalles Road

Gala apple trees frame Mt. Hood, Mt. Hood Organic Farms

processing the valley's forests for lumber as fast as they could be cut down. About this time, enterprising upper valley settlers began to dynamite and cut irrigation ditches to funnel the abundant water from glacier run-off to orchards.

In 1886, pioneer Peter Mohr, newly arrived from Germany, planted 400 apple trees on the east side of the lower valley near what is now Pine Grove. Mohr's orchard was probably the first commercial orchard planted on dry land in the Hood River Valley, relying solely on irrigation. Soon, orchards began to spring up all over the valley, thanks to a network of irrigation ditches criss-crossing the undulating terrain. Many of those original ditches provide the foundation for the Hood River Valley's modern irrigation network. Today, nearly 100 percent of the valley's orchards are irrigated.

By the early 1900s, the Hood River Valley was a patchwork quilt of apple orchards and strawberry fields. Many farmers would interplant strawberries between rows of fruit trees so they would have a saleable crop in the years before their apple trees began to bear fruit. The famous Clark's Seedling strawberry was grown and shipped from Hood River by the ton; in 1903, more than 90,000 crates of berries were shipped from the valley. Strawberry production tapered off when fruit trees matured and began shading out the low-lying strawberry plants. Eventually, apples overtook all other fruit production and became the Hood River Valley's top crop. By the second decade of the 1900s, apples from the valley had become famous well beyond the Northwest. Discriminating East Coast buyers favored Hood River Valley apples, and freight cars of fruit trundling out of the Hood River Depot garnered top dollar. Local fruit also began to be shipped to Europe, where the British favored the supreme

Newtown Pippin – which they called "saltwater apples" – grown beneath the slopes of Mt. Hood, named for their own British Naval Admiral Arthur Hood. Hood River Valley apples became so desirable that unscrupulous fruit vendors were known to label apples as such – and charge a premium price – even if the fruit had come from somewhere else.

The winter of 1919 forever changed the face of orcharding in the Hood River Valley. In December of that year, temperatures plunged to 27 degrees below zero. Many apple trees suffered such severe damage that entire orchards had to be uprooted and replaced. Many farmers, on the advice of the local agricultural extension agent from the state college in Corvallis, replaced their apple trees with hardier winter pears. In the years following the disastrous freeze, pear acreage slowly overtook that of apples. By the mid-1940s, pears were the primary Hood River Valley crop and it has remained that way ever since. Today, about 12,000 of the valley's 15,000 harvested acres of orchards are pears. About 1,500 acres are planted in apples, 1,100 acres in sweet cherries and about 60 acres in wine grapes.

Technology has advanced to help orchardists confront the whims of Mother Nature. In the 1970s, orchardists began installing fans amid their tree rows to help with frost prevention. On cold spring nights, the fans are cranked up to mix the warmer inversion layer with the cold air near the ground in order to prevent frost from damaging the budding trees. When the threat of a deeper cold looms, fans are used in conjunction with the more antiquated smudge pots – akin to stoves set up throughout an orchard to chase away the frost.

During the past few years orchardists in the valley, like independent farmers everywhere, have faced myriad challenges

Colorful tulips and cherry blossoms, Walton Orchards

Sorting cherries

more complex than those that nature presents in making ends meet. Imported fruit from South America and other regions has brought down the price of fruit grown in the valley. In addition, the value of the dollar has hurt the pear industry in world markets. Poor marketing efforts – especially when it comes to pears – have also contributed to lackluster sales.

Many Hood River Valley orchardists have met these challenges – especially the last one – head on in the past few years by coming up with creative ways to add value to their fruit. Third generation orcharding brothers Scott and Addison Webster started The Fruit Company four years ago as a way to boost flat sales from their 600-acre pear and apple orchard. With the Fruit Company, the Websters combine the old-fashioned – but always in fashion – quality of their Hood River Valley fruit with the modern wonders of the Internet and overnight delivery to sell their fruit all over the world. A wide assortment of gift boxes and baskets, ranging from whole boxes of ready-to-eat pears to "towers" filled with fruit, nuts, chocolate and other goodies, can be ordered online or over the phone for delivery anywhere, any time.

Gorge Delights was started three years ago by two long-time valley orcharding families in a similar effort to stimulate fruit sales. The company sells fresh sliced pears and apples in individual containers and in re-sealable bags for restaurants. The company recently partnered with the U.S. Department of Agriculture to produce a pear bar, a healthy snack bar made from a puree that contains the equivalent of two whole pears. Not only has Gorge Delights brought success to the orchardists who started it – not to mention delicious and healthful fruit to consumers – it is providing another sales alternative to other valley pear and apple growers.

Second generation orchardists Rick and Bette Benjamin took a long-time family hobby – making dried fruit from pears taken off the packing line because of imperfections – and started the Hood River Dried Fruit Company. They now make dried pears and apples, as well as pear leather and – a customer favorite – chocolate-dipped pear slices. They are successfully marketing their product in the Hood River Valley and other select locations in the Northwest, and shipping it around the world via orders from their website.

Local orchardist John Jacobson has put his own altruistic twist on value-added fruit. Jacobson, who turned his 60-acre apple and pear orchard into an organic farm in the late 1980s, has partnered with grocery store chains in Portland and the Columbia Gorge to sell his fruit and give the profits to local school programs. Another organic farm, Columbia Gorge Organics, got into the value-added business several years ago when its owner-brothers began making juices from their organic fruit. Columbia Gorge Organics now sells an entire organic juice line up and down the West Coast.

And nearly all Hood River Valley growers are tapping in to the growth in agri-tourism. The Hood River Valley Fruit Loop was born in recent years as a direct result of this. The Fruit Loop is a 35-mile driving route (or bike route, if you're so inclined!) that starts in Hood River and winds up the east side of the valley on Highway 35 before looping through Parkdale and back down the west side of the valley on Highway 281, the Dee Highway. The Loop takes visitors past two dozen orchards, fruit stands, U-pick farms, wineries, a plant nursery, an alpaca farm and the valley's only chestnut farm. Along with fresh fruit and farm products for sale along the route, farms offer a variety of options

Smudge pots protect pear orchard from frost

The view on a cold morning

Chestnuts, Nutquacker Farms

Pumpkin Fun Land, Rasmussen Farms

49

Pine Grove Vineyard in the fall

Riesling grapes, Pine Grove Vineyard

Farm workers celebrate the harvest, Kirby Orchards

Impromptu dancing at Fiesta Days in Odell

to visitors, from orchard tours to picking your own fruit to wine tastings – and even a chance to "work" on an orchard.

The Fruit Loop attracts thousands of visitors during the valley's annual Blossom Festival, held each year during the third weekend in April. A 50-year-old tradition, Blossom Festival is a celebration of the bounty of the Hood River Valley that coincides with the spring blossoming of the pear and apple trees. The valley is an explosion of pink and white blossoms during the weekend, attracting visitors from around the Northwest and beyond. The Fruit Loop provides a perfect way to view the blossoms and get a taste – literally – of what this valley is all about. Driving or biking the Loop also offers a chance to visit the quaint valley communities that were established in Hood River's early years when travel from upper valley orchards to Hood River was more difficult. Pine Grove, Odell, Mt. Hood and Parkdale all played important roles historically, and continue to add their own flavor to life in the valley.

Many other special events throughout the year also highlight the Fruit Loop and its member farms. The Pear & Wine Festival, held each May, is a weekend-long celebration of the valley's most famous product along with wines from more than a dozen of Oregon's top wineries – including local vintners from the Hood River Valley. Cooking demonstrations, pairings of pears and complementary foods, and specialty pear products – including pear cider and sherry and pear pie – help put the spotlight on the many varieties of the valley's most famous fruit.

Other special events are held at individual orchards throughout the summer and fall. Rasmussen Farms, which has been catering to visitors since 1963, hosts a variety of events at its Pine Grove orchard. The farm's Summer Sensations, in June, coincides with the strawberry season and features U-pick and ready-picked berries and other family activities – including the strawberry shot put. Pumpkin Funland, in October, is known around the Northwest as a must-see for the more than 50 whimsical scenes created with pumpkins, as well as a corn maze and other fun for kids and families.

Gravenstein Apple Days takes place in August at several orchards along the Fruit Loop. Gravensteins are considered one of the best apples for cooking, and the weekend-long celebration highlights everything from apple pies and apple sauce to caramel apples and apple dumplings.

Fiesta Days, held at Kiyokawa Orchards in October, celebrates the contributions Hispanics have made to orcharding in the Hood River Valley. Festivities include traditional Mexican food, Mariachi bands and piñata contests. Self-guided tours of the orchard provide a great look at an orchard during the peak of the harvest season. The Kiyokawas, third generation Japanese American orchardists, also give tours that offer insights into their own family history in the valley as well as an historical overview of Hood River Valley orcharding.

The Hood River Valley's renowned Harvest Fest is held during one of the last weekends in October. A decades-old tradition, the festival celebrates the bounty of the Hood River Valley at the end of the harvest season. The Hood River Expo Center and its grounds are filled with food and craft booths, and farm fresh produce is available in great abundance.

Special farm events continue even after the traditional fall harvest is over. At Nutquacker Farms, the valley's first chestnut farm, November ushers in the season of ripening Colossal Chestnuts. The farm's Italian Style Chestnut Roast celebrates the

Delicious pies at Apple Valley Country Store

Bountiful harvest

Pears grown in brandy bottles at McCurdy Farms for Clear Creek Distillery

Part of the diversity, Warm Springs Native American maidens

Hood River Equestrian Classic held each June

Opposite: Hood River 4th of July fireworks

longstanding Italian tradition of pairing chestnuts and red wine. According to custom, the chestnuts are roasted, peeled and dropped into a glass of wine. The chestnut's earthy flavor and aroma mingle with the fruitiness of the wine to create a distinct flavor. The farm's specialty, Colossal Chestnuts, are a Japanese-European hybrid developed for their large size, sweetness and ease of peeling – and they go nicely with the featured Hood River Valley wines.

Another not-to-be-missed highlight of the valley's fruit industry is the orchard where more than 2,500 pears are grown inside glass bottles. Portland's Clear Creek Distillery, run by a Hood River Valley native, makes its famous "pear-in-the-bottle" eau-de-vie with pears grown on McCurdy Farms. In the spring, bottles are placed over tiny pears just before they get too big to fit through the neck. The bottles are tied onto the trees neck down so water can drain out. At harvest time the bottles and their mature pears are taken to the distillery where they become the specialty spirit sold around the world. An orchard tour of pears growing in bottles is an experience not soon forgotten!

Interest in the Hood River Valley's farms and fruit continues to grow as cities become more crowded and urbanites feel increasingly disconnected from the land. Man's reliance on nature and bond with the earth is felt nowhere more strongly than on the farms and orchards of the valley, where the forces of climate and geology continue to make their presence known.

Opposite: High on the cliff, the Columbia Gorge Hotel with Mt. Hood backdrop

The sternwheeler, Columbia Gorge, *a great way to view the Columbia River Cross Channel Swim, each Labor Day*

Swimmers in the Columbia River Cross Channel Swim

Thomas the Tank visits Hood River

Mt. Hood Scenic Railroad travels up the valley during pear bloom

Mike's Ice Cream, Hood River

Apple Valley Country Store

Outrigger Canoe Race, Gorge Games

Nike Trail Run, Gorge Games

Kayak Race, Gorge Games

Full Sail Ale, Cycle Oregon Team nears finish line

CHAPTER 6

HOLA AND SAYONARA

Not only did fruit bring prosperity to the Hood River Valley, it brought diversity as well, dating back to the earliest settlers. As people began to migrate to the valley, they naturally sent news back to where they'd come from encouraging friends and relatives to join them. By the early 1880s, a group of German families had settled in the Pine Grove area, bringing their own traditions and culture to the valley. Similarly, a couple of Finnish families who settled in the 1890s in the Oak Grove area, across the valley from Pine Grove, were soon followed by others from Finland drawn to the valley for its fruit growing potential. Along with the long-held Finnish tradition of sauna, the Finns contributed much in the way of their mountaineering background and expertise to the expanding climbing and mountain rescue communities. Nearly half of the founding members of the Crag Rats were Finns.

By the late 1890s, Japanese had begun to arrive in the valley. Thousands of Japanese had flocked to the U.S. to help build the railroads of the West during the latter 1800s, including the tracks that ran through the Columbia Gorge. Many stayed in the area when construction began on the Mt. Hood Railroad in 1905. During slow times, and after the railroad was completed – first to Dee and later to Parkdale – many Japanese went to work on orchards or in the valley's lumber mills. Through hard work, many Japanese went from laborer to land-owner and by the 1920s, there were many successful Japanese orchardists in the valley. Today, some of the area's most respected multi-generation family orchards are owned by Japanese whose ancestors literally helped build the Hood River Valley.

During and after World War II, Hispanics began trickling into the valley to work on the orchards as farm labor. Most of them were migrant workers at first, living here from spring to fall during the height of the fruit growing and picking season. During the past couple of decades, however, more of them began staying year-round, finding work at packing houses and elsewhere to get them through the off-season. They began sending for their families south of the border, or starting families here. Today, one-quarter of the valley's population is Hispanic. While many still work in agriculture, they have branched into other facets of the community as well – working in local industries, in the service sector and in health care. Members of one of the earliest Hispanic families to settle in the valley started Juanita's Fine Foods, which makes tortillas and other Mexican foods from its headquarters in Pine Grove. The business is one of the most successful manufacturers in the valley. A decade ago, only a handful of Hispanic students graduated from the local high school. Now, nearly thirty percent of the high school's graduating class each year is Hispanic.

The ethnic diversity in the Hood River Valley has given rise to popular and much-anticipated cultural events that draw together the whole community. Every March local Finns celebrate St. Uhro's Day in grand – and hilarious – style. St. Uhro is a fictional Finnish saint who supposedly drove the grasshoppers out of Finland and into Ireland, thus saving the grape harvest. Local Finns gather for the crowning of the new queen (who isn't necessarily female), then parade through town in an assortment of irreverent outfits and vehicles in varying shades of purple and lime green. The parade ends in front of City Hall where the ritual "Changing of the Guard" takes place – a ceremony that involves

The beautiful Hood River Inn

St. Uhro's Day Parade

The famous International Museum of Carousel Art

Holiday lights at the historic Columbia Gorge Hotel

stripping from winter garments down to underwear, thus officially ushering in spring. The St. Uhro's celebration has gained fame even beyond Hood River – in 1978, local Finns persuaded Oregon's governor to officially proclaim March 16th, St. Uhro's Day – and it is a much-loved event that brings out crowds all along the parade route.

Another popular annual event is the Fiesta Celebration. Held at the fairgrounds, the September gathering celebrates Hispanic culture with folk dances, traditional Mexican food and arts and crafts. The growing prominence of Hispanic culture in the valley is also evident in the many quinceañeras taking place year round. A traditional Latin American celebration of a girl's 15th birthday, a quinceañera is often a day-long event that includes much preparation, a church ceremony and a party for hundreds that lasts late into the night. The celebrations can be seen often on weekends, as participants mingle in their finery outside St. Mary's Catholic Church, or make their way through town in car caravans. The quinceañeras and other cultural traditions highlight the rich diversity here and remind us that, when it comes to people, the "whole" of the Hood River Valley is greater than the sum of its parts.

CHAPTER 7

MODERN DAY EMIGRANTS

The perpetual attraction of the Hood River Valley to "emigrants" surged again in the 1980s. The new sport of windsurfing had recently emerged on the beaches of California, and "boardheads" in search of wind and water discovered a magical place with a heavenly combination of the two called Hood River, Oregon.

Wind had long been a nuisance in Hood River and the valley. Blowing steadily out of the west from spring through fall, wind gets literally sucked from low pressure systems at the coast to the high pressure of the desert, picking up speed as it funnels through the high walls of the Gorge. Since the earliest white settlers came to the valley – and long before that – the wind was an ever-present annoyance, whisking off men's hats and whipping ladies' skirts. Rows of poplars were sometimes planted to the west of orchards to serve as windbreaks. Close-set shrubs would provide some relief to backyards. But the wind never ceased and locals accepted it as part of life in Hood River.

When windsurfers heard about the great windy river in Oregon and came to check it out, they discovered another delight: the Columbia flowed west to the ocean, against the wind blowing east toward the desert. This created big swells and even breaking waves on the wide river, making for challenging conditions unlike those found anywhere in the world. Word quickly spread and a sports town was born.

Windsurfers began to streaming into town and by the early 1990s the population of Hood River was swelling to nearly double its 5,000 residents during the summer months. Along with the windsurfers, an influx of money blew into town – a

Downtown Hood River

Hood River farm on Eastside Road

73

timely windfall as most of Hood River's once-thriving fruit canneries had closed and the booming timber industry in the valley was on the wane. Dilapidated store fronts were spruced up and turned into windsurfing shops. Restaurants and boutiques sprang up to cater to the crowds. Windsurfing competitions during the summer that attracted competitors from around the world put Hood River on the map for the first time since the early days of the fruit boom in the valley.

By the mid-1990s, sports enthusiasts were discovering that Hood River and the valley had lots more to offer than just windsurfing. Mountain biking on the valley's trails and logging roads and kayaking on the rivers spilling from the Cascades became huge draws in themselves. In 1996, a week-long sports festival highlighting nearly a dozen outdoor sports was launched in Hood River, and the Gorge Games has since become one of the premier summer events in the Northwest. Media coverage of the Games has spurred further growth in tourism.

The emergence of Hood River as a tourist destination has evolved in the past few years. Windsurfing and other outdoor sports still take center stage during the summer, but visitors of all persuasions now flock to town from spring through fall. A respected artists' community has sprung up, evidenced by the many galleries in town that feature work by local artisans. Similarly, a large number of musicians and bands have taken root here. The combination has spawned a monthly cultural gathering called First Friday, where local downtown businesses stay open all evening on the first Friday of each month, each one showcasing different artists and musicians. The festive event draws people to town from all around the valley; even in the off-season when tourist numbers are low, it's hard to find a parking space anywhere near downtown on the first Friday evening of the month.

Visitors come to experience the vibrant fruit industry, and for many other attractions as well. The historic Mt. Hood Railroad draws thousands of visitors each year for its excursion trains that take passengers up the valley along the same rails that began transporting lumber and fruit – and pioneering valley settlers – nearly 100 years ago. The International Museum of Carousel Art attracts visitors for the mere curiosity of it: it houses the largest collection of historic carousel figures in the world, as well as restored carousels from around the country and as far away as Europe. Hood River is a major stop for tour boats plying the Columbia – including the replica sternwheelers that let passengers experience what it was like when paddle boats were the main mode of transportation through the Columbia Gorge. An annual equestrian competition held in June, the Hood River Classic, has grown into one of the premier horse shows in the Northwest. Yet another annual competition of sorts, the Roy Webster Cross Channel Swim – named after the orchardist who started it in 1946 – brings water lovers from around the region to swim across the mighty Columbia each Labor Day. Activities like golfing, sailboating and even birdwatching take on new meaning here with the breathtaking backdrops of the Hood River Valley and the Columbia Gorge.

Downtown Hood River has been revitalized during the past decade. Power lines were placed below ground and many historic buildings restored to their original splendor. Visitors can take a self-guided walking tour of the Downtown Historic District. Highlights are the old Mt. Hood Hotel, built in 1912 and now called the Hood River Hotel; the Craftsman style railroad

Teeing off at Indian Creek Golf Club with Mt. Adams in background

A beautiful view of Mt. Hood and the Hood River Valley

depot built in 1911 by the O.W.R.& N. Company Railroad, now operated by the Mt. Hood Railroad; and the Union Building built in 1905, the oldest warehouse associated with the fruit industry in Hood River. Many old homes in town dating to the late 1800s and early 1900s have been restored as well, and a flurry of new construction has given parts of town a whole new look.

As windsurfers and other newcomers settled in Hood River in the 1980s and '90s, jobs were scarce and many became entrepreneurs simply in order to live here. Some of those once-fledgling companies are now thriving businesses in Hood River, ranging from outdoor apparel companies to software firms. Several windsurfing industry companies relocated to Hood River and, along with new ones begun here, continue to be an important part of the economy.

The growth of Hood River and the valley over the past couple of decades has been steady, and sometimes bittersweet for those who want it to remain "undiscovered." But as new lifestyles nestle alongside old ones, the Hood River Valley has – yet again – been made richer. Everyone who is drawn here, whether to visit or to live, shares a common passion for this place. We all know that the valley's abundance – from the fruit and scenery to the recreation and the people themselves – is inextricably linked to the past. And it is up to all of us to make sure that the Hood River Valley, this treasure of the earth, will continue to stir passion in people's souls for a long, long time to come.

ABOUT THE AUTHOR

JANET COOK, a native of Boulder, Colorado, arrived in Hood River 13 years ago intending to spend a summer learning to windsurf. Aside from a few brief leaves of absence, she's been there ever since. She and her husband, Peter Hixson, enjoy the laid-back lifestyle of the Hood River Valley, and the abundance of "plenty" it offers in everything from recreation to beauty to gastronomic delights. Janet is a staff writer for the *Hood River News*, where she writes feature stories about the people and places that make the Hood River Valley perpetually intriguing. She is a 1988 graduate of Lewis & Clark College in Portland, and a 1994 graduate of Syracuse University, where she received a master's degree in journalism. Since joining the *Hood River News* in 1997, she has won numerous regional and national awards for her writing.

ABOUT THE PHOTOGRAPHER

PETER MARBACH resides in Hood River with his wife, Lorena, and daughter, Sofia. Peter's passion for the outdoors began in earnest in the 1980's by hiking the lengths of the Appalachian Trail, Pacific Crest Trail, and The Pennine Way in Great Britain.

His first book with Beautiful America, *OREGON HARVEST*, received critical acclaim for documenting the beauty of Oregon's farm country and the people who work the land.

Peter's photography has appeared in numerous national publications. His stock collections of wilderness and agricultural landscapes has been used in calendars, books, magazines and advertising. Several of his award winning farmscapes are part of a permanent collection at Oregon State University's Art About Agriculture Exhibit.

He has published several fine art posters, including three consecutive Mt. Hood Jazz Festival Commemorative prints and his most recent, "Morning At Mount Hood." More information on Peter can be found at www.petermarbachphotography.com.

Mt. Hood at sunset

Rear cover: The beautiful earthenware from Mystic Mud Studio, Hood River